Happy Mother's Day Notebook: The Perfect Gift Book For Mom
Mother's Day Gift Ideas
Paperback ISBN: 978-1-989733-20-2
 Cover Design by Sharon Purtill

www.ingramcontent.com/pod-product-compliance
Lightning Source LLC
Chambersburg PA
CBHW070515200726
48293CB00007B/2555